When We Wake We Think We're Whalers from Eden

Bob Beagrie

Stairwell Books //

Published by Stairwell Books
161 Lowther Street
York, YO31 7LZ

www.stairwellbooks.co.uk
@stairwellbooks

ISBN: 978-1-913432-27-0
Layout: Alan Gillott
Cover image: 'Penumbra' by Gail Henderson, 2000. Mixed media on
paper, 152.4 x 121.9 cm. Photograph by Elizabeth Hall

Acknowledgements

Thanks to the editors of the following publications in which some of the poems from this collection first appeared:

New Boots & Pantisocracies, Abridged, New Reader Magazine, Valiant Scribe, Stepaway Magazine, Dreich, Strands, Boyne Berries, The Pangolin Review, The Lockdown Project and *Covid and Poetry.*

"Thus each of us had to be content to live only for the day, alone under the vast indifference of the sky."

Albert Camus, *The Plague*

Table of Contents

Gaming with the Galaxy

You make a dash to the corner shop
To pick up a four pack of toilet roll,
Having realised you're down
To the last two straggled sheets
Glued to the cardboard tube and
Obviously they're not going to do.

Two teenage girls sweep by like
Empty crisp packets in the wind,
Giggling at the fun of being alive
And young, scattering infectious
Crumbs of carelessness into puddles
Of clogged up drains, dodge around
Parked cars in a game of Tag-You-Stink.

"You stink!" one shrieks as she passes
On the terrible contagion by touching
Her best friend's coated shoulder, who
Momentarily melts like a cheap candle
Before rocketing after her to give it back.

You shudder as if someone has stepped
On your grave but it's a weakly interactive
Massive particle moving through you,
Passing indiscriminately through the matter
Of your corporeal form and the darting
Bouncing, giggling bodies of the two girls,
On its spectral trip across the universe
Echoing two words to all your inner spaces,
"You stink. You stink. You stink. You stink." ⁄⁄

Storm in a Pothole

See how that bus is towing clouds
    across the flyover
like party balloons and streamers
    as if a bride and groom
are on board waving in a blizzard
    of cheesy grins and confetti,
while the radio warns us
    another storm is about to hit
riding in on the tail of the last
    that set the rivers loose
to roam willy-nilly wherever
    they wanted, looting whatever
they could reach, a riot, a movement
of mass disobedience,
and isn't that Thunder and Lightening
    loitering at the next stop
watching the idling traffic through
the Perspex windows
of the shelter like two bored teenagers
    on a first awkward date
with nowhere to go or nothing much
    to do apart from taking the piss
out of anyone and everything they see:
    the darkening sky
    the bridge
    the river quivering
in anticipation at its chance
    to slip its leash again,
"Let's play knocky-knocky-hide-o!" the river spits.
You'd think it was time it grew up and got a life.
    Thunder shrugs,
    Lightening sparks up a spliff.
The lights turn green, we drive into the rain. ⁄⁄

Blowing Out

My Dad is building a wall. Twirling bricks in the air,
bedding them down in a quarter-bond, flicking the trowel
to lay a mat of fresh darbo. With one brick after the next in
a cheeky wink of an eye the edifice rises and so does the
scaffold but no one can tell what he's building. He has
abandoned the architect's plans. A loose crowd has
gathered, observing Social Distancing, as speculations
spread: he's building a new Tower of Babel, it's the new
walls of Jericho, Jerusalem, Kingdom Come, he's making a
Stairway to Heaven, it's a folly, it's a marvel, it's a
sanatorium free from the sickness, it's a dam to stop both
tide and time, he's building a Neverland where anything
goes.

You move through the space trying to touch as little as
possible, and would, if you could, lighten yourself so your
feet could lift a few inches from the floor. Over the last few
days we have all been made more attentive to the auras
that surround us, our own personal biospheres of electro-
magnetic energy. Even if most can't see them, as some
more mystically attuned people claim to, we recognise their
potentially infectious existence.

And the ventilator makes another regular sigh. Your mind
is a sanitised side room full of bleeps and whirrs where the
familiar names of things melt and orientations blur. The
white tiled floor is the wall at your back, a compact and
undeniable once-upon-a-time, too solid and certain to look
at with more than a furtive glance. The ceiling's expanse is
the hazy horizon line where the North Sea kisses the foot
of the sky, toward which you have tossed how many
memories with an expert flick of the wrist? The pane of
glass into the ward is a TV screen showing a soap opera
you assumed you inhabited, filling the void with all of
those familiar roles and routines.

And the ventilator makes another regular sigh, a slow
mechanical exhalation. You know, Nirvana literally means
'blowing out', an emptying, a quenching, a sluicing of self
into śūnyatā through the gates of ten thousand things:
magpie hoards, tower blocks, get well cards, daisy chains,
fish gills and razor blades, the sightless eyes of a forest of
needles through which a caravan of dromedaries trudge
toward a sunset, their two-toed splayed feet sinking into
dust dunes of lost civilisations, misplaced wedding rings,
rune casts, pollen coated bee fur, shipping forecasts,
Michael Portillo's voluminous nostrils, the signatures
drying on birth and death certificates and Yul Bryner
intoning, Etcetera, etcetera etcetera!

And the ventilator makes another regular sigh to the
bleeps, chirps and whirs of the electronic menagerie. Your
blood flows through transparent tubes into the dialysis
machine and back into your body, a conservatory for your
circulatory system. My Dad is building his miraculous wall
and no one can guess what it's part of, but he looks so
much younger than he should. Outside the sealed room of
your sedated mind the world serpent constricts its coils and
its freshly brewed venom transmits between persons, more
infectious than a giggle in school assembly, as paranoid
and undiscerning as a lynch mob in the grip of mass
hysteria, as profound and transformational as love released
from the moorings of desire. ⁄⁄

Mutability in a State of Emergency

The Pre-Assessment waiting room is quiet today, hardly surprising given the situation, essential procedures only. The radio is playing 'People Call Me a Space Cowboy' and the receptionist is unusually short, so much so that only her upper forehead and hairline crest the desk, but its bobbing along to the tune and she seems happy enough despite the State of Emergency. Still, we all need to compartmentalise our fears and concerns or else panic will break its banks and drown us.

In the opposite seat to me a Cro-Magnon man sits wearing a pale blue, medical face mask, it looks like a muzzle to stop him from snarling and biting. He is infected by wolves, a kind of multiple lychanthropy where a whole pack has taken up residence in his struggle-hardened body, trotting along veins, loping through arteries, padding around the ridges and crevasses of his skeleton, howling through his eyes. Occasionally he shakes his head as if to scare away an unbidden thought or disturb a persistent fly that has taken a fancy to his scent.

The Cro-Magnon man is called Simon, the receptionist called his name and gave him a form to fill out before disappearing again behind her counter but he is not even attempting to add any details. He just stares at it or through it with his howling eyes. The white sheet becoming a snow filled, wind-swept tundra where a straggled line of wolves weave toward a rise known by the local tribes as Mammoth Ridge.

The small receptionist asks if he is alright, "You alright Simon?' she says and tells him she'll take the form once it's done. Her disembodied voice drifts like a flurry of snowflakes from behind her counter. Simon the Cro-Magnon looks around as if sniffing the air for a hint of unseen prey or predator and then spots me with a start as if I have, just this instant, teleported onto the green plastic chair beside a water cooler with a pink sticker on it saying it's an angel and asks us to make a wish.

"You alright mate?" Simon enquires from behind his muzzle, which billows with the breath of each word, as if his wolves are trying to escape from his mouth and spread their lupine bacterium. I nod and give him a wary half smile as Steve Miller confesses to being a joker, a smoker, a midnight toker, and I say, "Yeah, just about. Crazy days eh?" but he just shakes his head and looks back at his form, speechless. ⁄⁄

The New Rules to Abide By

Now that all distances have vanished, content yourself
with nooks and crannies, where the wild hunt goes on for
woodlice, spiders and silver fish.

Listen to the sounds of your own voice, hum a tune to test
how the different rooms of your house change the timber
and tone.

Distrust the news from the mainstream, twiddle your
thumbs and shoo your ghosts out to roam the emptied
streets.

They have been learning obscure languages to glean the
truth from the horse's mouth, from the puppet play of
crows, the deeper secrets of stone.

When they return they will gather in the back bedroom to
enact their pantomimes, you will need a torch or a candle
at least to watch their shadow plays

And you will weep a little from the ache and longing for
what you always assumed was real, the things you took for
granted; things like places, comings and goings, meetings
and encounters, the uninhibited touch of others.

Whenever you take the plunge to venture out your solitary
footsteps insist on stretching before you then lagging
behind, they'll sweep one way then the other with the
fluidity of tides.

Inmates will watch you with suspicion through their
windows and the bolder sort may demand you justify what
is essential.

Queuing is a new art form of occupying silences, observing proximities and scouring the gaps on the supermarket shelves.

Key Workers have become the envy of all, kings and queens of purpose, who still possess minutes, hours, even days of the week.

Everyone else marks the passage of time through the ritual washing of hands, holidaying in the kitchen then voyaging across the Great Laminate Plains in search of the remote control.

Patience is the new black and should be decorated as you would a Christmas Tree with fairy lights and baubles, place presents at its feet and worship it as your saviour.

Dismiss urban myths of warlords who live in fortresses of toilet rolls and who eat nothing but pasta, some of them supposedly have unicorns in their gardens adorned in the flags of old nation states.

Within your cocoon you must digest yourself into protein-rich soup, disintegrating all of your tissues except for the imaginal discs, which use the goo of your previous existence to fuel the rapid cell division required to undergo a radical transformation into a new physical form and a somewhat different personality after instances which would normally result in death. //

The Quickening

With restrictions on free movement set and enforced
explorers ventured in alternative directions of discovery.

Many began voyages into the past;
their own, their family's bloodline,
or into the folds of larger historical trajectories.

Those around them noticed how they began
to fade from the present, gradually dissipating,
dissolving into all of those accumulated yesterdays.

Others blended with music and travelled
along waves of sound, they glowed
with the brief, bright lustre of a carillon
before burning out, crumbling to conical piles of dust.

Others endeavoured to chart the territories of stillness,
learning to overcome the body's desire for action,
its rampant restlessness and its love of kinetics
and eventually they entered The Palace of Placidity.

Others explored the dynamics of exercise
in limited, locked down spaces, filling the rooms
with volatile gesture, bringing their bodily vibrations
to such a pitch they shook themselves apart;
you'd be forgiven for mistaking them for smoke.

There were some who poured themselves
into the intricacies of new pastimes, some cooked
and served themselves up to the day after tomorrow
and there were even those who untangled themselves
by teasing out a thread, tugging it free, wandering
through the labyrinth while reeling themselves out.

And so this was how the last explorers during
The Great Isolation disappeared into extinction,
flowing one by one out of time. ⁄⁄

Two Meters

The safety zone contains five straggly weeds
Seven cigarette butts in a drift of dandelion fluff
Your squat fidgeting shadow on its phone
The lilt of speech in a language I've never learned
A pale splodge of dried chewing gum
Pulsating unease and a polite smile returned
Nostalgia for the way we used to live, not so long ago
Air that's noticeably cleaner to breathe
The chirp, tweet and whistle of small concealed birds
Suspect droplets of moisture, musings on the weather
A passing police officer's measuring stare
Suspicions of flouting the rules of the lock-down
Worries around loved ones and the lack of an income
Possibilities for a different kind of future. ⁄⁄

Meds

Ten of us pretending to be sick dicky birds sitting on the
chemist wall. Most minding their own business and
whiling out the wait and it feels good to have the sun
warming the back of our necks though there's still a chill in
the wind. We observe the two metre rule because we are
responsible dicky birds and fear the vapours from each
other's beaks. But just around the corner a gaggle of
teenagers are climbing all over the scaffolding surrounding
Sabai Thai Massage, closed as it's unessential.

The Chemists are only letting two in at a time, one in and
one out, but apologise for any inconvenience. It says that
on a sign taped beside the door. I see a hectic ambulance
hurtling along the road, blue lights and sirens fill our
heads. Someone sicker than us ten pretend sick dicky
birds. Each of us are washed in electric blues then it's gone.
We shuffle along.

Dandelions populate the scruffy little lawn grinning at the
sun around flagless poles. Flags are non-essential in this
No Mans' Limbo Land but the poles quiver in the wind and
their shadows lounge across the pavement. We hold onto
titbits of empathy although trust has been trimmed to a
crew cut and most people are looking for someone to blame.
Trust is the scaffold supporting Sabai Thai Massage.
Blame is the gang of kids playing monkeys without any
thought of danger. They don't even bother keeping their
distance from each other. They're still in love with colour.
We shuffle along.

Whenever someone wanders toward the doors one of us will
yell, "There's a queue!" We, who make up the queue, have
bonded in solidarity. We are the queue. You tell me the
Lidl near you was ram-raided last night. You tell me you
were blown up in the Falklands, show me the scars on your
legs to prove it. Say it still gives you jip in the Winter but

13

the medication is for the missus. Why is it taking so long if they're already made up? I tell you absolutely nothing about me but you don't seem to mind. We shuffle up and I reach the front of the queue.

One of the staff comes out and announces to us ten pretend sick dicky birds they're closing for lunch, sorry but we'll have to wait or come back in an hour, then she pulls the shutters down. We've nowhere to shuffle except off.

No way I'm giving up my place at the front of the queue. You won't be budging either. We nest down for the wait. Look at the colours behind our eyelids, the lingering blue, hectic and hurtling. Count the dandelions on the lawn basking in the sun. Watch how the shadows of the flagpoles creep closer like an accusing finger. ⁄⁄

When We Wake We Think We're Whalers From Eden

So this is paradise? So this is Eden? The streams flow from
our taps. I must be Adam. Your name must be Eve or else
Helpmeet. We water spider plants on the shelves. Share
the apples from the fruit bowl. Each morning you take a
bath where you sometimes cry at the thought of our
imprisonment. I patrol the perimeter. We cannot go out
into the world and explore the woods or the beach, seek out
friends and family. The door is guarded by Simon Templar,
unruffled by any of our pleas and arguments.

How long is our sentence? When were we press-ganged?
Time flows from our taps. I must be all but dust by now.
You must be burnt bone or soot-stained wood. We watch
reruns of Kojak on daytime TV. Share funny memes from
our news-feeds. Each afternoon we practice Qi Gong and
sometimes sigh at the view from our porthole. Our breaths
fog the glass. We cannot dig our way out like the Tunnel
King in The Great Escape, but we share his
claustrophobia. Why has the world outside our Eden grown
quiet?

How long do you think this will last? What will it be like
when it's over? Days drain down the plughole. We must try
to remain positive. We water our reasons for self-isolation.
Share our doubts about the News we're force fed. Each
evening we play backgammon and sometimes we say 'I love
you' and 'Love you back'. I pour you a glass of wine. We
cannot drink our way out of these four walls, we both know
you're too vulnerable to be out and about especially with
this new plague doing the rounds of the Earth.

So, are you still here? After all these years? The fire burns
strings of unspoken words. We must remember who we
were. We water our memories with old Polaroids. Share
our sexual fantasies for kicks. Each night-time we lie

beside one another, under the quilt and travel through dream-lands. You patrol the circumference of my sleep. Our breaths surface and dive like a pod of whales crossing the Atlantic and somewhere behind them sails The Pequod, fanaticism and whole dark history of whaling. ⁄⁄

On Touch

It was such an easy thing to do
and is the hardest to lose.

Today we met, not bumped into, someone
(that, now, would be inexcusable)

and we stood at a required distance,
and she burst into tears

which set you off crying too,
because you could not exchange a simple hug,

rub cheeks and hold one another in place,
and feel the momentary grounding of each other

in a physical recognition of shared battles.
How, while a swarm of midges clouded

over the brackish waters of the beck,
words of tenderness tried their best

to make up for the trust of the touchy-feely,
leaving us grateful, though a little diminished.

Somehow virtual. ⁄⁄

Shadowlands

"Do not fear to suffer; - cares sink back
Into the earth again from their heaviness;
Heavy are the mountains, heavy are the seas."
    Rainer Maria Rilke, *Sonnets to Orpheus*

It became necessary to suspend all sense of disbelief,
there was no tree on which to hang your scepticism
like damp laundry on a washing line, socks, panties
waving in a sharp sea-breeze, one that's travelled miles

to say hello to our rootedness, but even that seemed
like a vague imago from before, just part and parcel
of false memory syndrome. Sure there was still wind
but how many of us could feel it given the symptoms?

I take what I'm allotted and wrap the house around me
like a shawl, thankful for its warmth and shelter,
the way it acts as an anchor, stops us drifting down
the tidal river, between the turbines and out to sea.

Especially while you're healing, in the tender-wince
of waiting for bruises to bloom, a bell-flower bouquet
we'll forget to set in a vase of water by the window,
ends up crumbling dried heads between our fingers. ⁄⁄

18

Pantheion

"Thrill with lissom lust of the light,
O man! My man!
Come careering out of the night
Of Pan! Io Pan!"
 Aleister Crowley, *Hymn to Pan*

They say the goats of the Great Worm have come careering down off its shoulders to rampage around the deserted town and live deliciously.

Footage of the boisterous trip was shown on the Evening News, their creamy fleeces a bubbling splurt of surf spilling through people's gardens and across the roads ignoring Give Way signs, they nibbled the hedges and flowers beds, climbed on walls, town benches, danced on tables in abandoned beer gardens, and their horns scraped against trees and keyed parked cars, rattled against gates to make their capricious music, obviously having a whale of a time while the townsfolk wait out their quarantine, penned in restless living rooms.

The footage shown was filmed during the day but after nightfall the mood of these shaggy, insatiable marauders alters. They have taken to lighting candles and placing them between their horns while staring into the windows of people's homes, licking their lips, whispering dark delights of living a life of lusty abandon. They tap their horns against the double glazing, rub their cheeks against brass door handles, snuffle wild promises through letterboxes, and prance through sleepers' keratin dreams bleating 'Once upon a time you were as free as me, let those memories stir up a perfect storm. Come out to play, let's swallow the dawn.'

With each passing day their numbers grow. ⚕

Dies Irae

The vacant kirk clings to foundations
with iron pins riven through palms
of faith to resist reversals
of random gravities, days shaken
in a dice-pot then spilled
to form fresh readings
raptor sky-swirl seeking rapture,
catkins dangle – ropes to glory;
this round ends the next begins,
so pay your tithe if you want in;
the river wakes, takes to wing,
toted like a new-born
on its palanquin
by cardinal water fowl
in singing procession,
circling wider over sand and sea,
their evening requiem:
Day of wrath and doom impending
Heaven and earth in ashes ending. ✍

Rub-a-dub-dub

How suspect are our bodies and their fluids,
dressed up and contained for the day ahead,
our essential trip out to catch a shred of Vitamin D
and replenish our stockpile from Tesco Express
which now thinks it's Ikea with its arrows on the floor
to guide us around the aisles in the designated route –
woe betide anyone who dares backtrack for milk. Yes,
these beautiful body-works that betray us look pretty
normal as our personalised convertibles, accessorized
and stamped by the mileage, all the usual wear
and tear, but some have been twokked by joyriders
disguised as our ordinary souls. We all know it
but don't have a clue as to who, so must suspect
everyone. The spy in the brain watches through
each and every eye, and we are all informers, judges
jurors and would-be executioners given half a chance. ⫽

Keeping Vigil

...or else this quiet, sun-soaked corner of the yard is the
outer edge of the universe, the clematis leaves jiggling,
trying to find purchase on the wall and scale it, cow bell
pegged above the gate rings thrice and somewhere at the
centre of things decisions are made. But not here, the wind
didn't decide to ring the bell nor this sunlight choose to
spill, though it warms bare arms and is welcome. Beyond
the wall the town goes on though at a slower pace this
Spring. It is the second day and I am holding my breath for
the third, wondering if it will come. Will the tomb open and
our man emerge, bright as a button? We love life and
maybe he will ask for his back. I knew someone who knew
someone who met him once, this man of peace who claimed
we all have a hole in our hearts; that's the spot where
solace can seed, or something like that. There are car horns
in the distance and occasional birdsong, although it's still
too early for eggshells to crack. The cow bell's dull clang is
soothing desire to do anything. It stills my nerves. I think
of swans gliding without a ripple on the river like
marshmallow hearts, melting reflections. There is nothing
to do but wait, remain awake and stoke contentment to
stay within the confines of this domicile, or else... ⁄⁄

A Hypernormalized Fairytale

Fleeing from the virus of virtual war planes
We found a wild forest lost inside a bus stop
Devoted sister and my sweet silent brother
Always on his telephone disconnected
From anything beyond the lit-up screen –
Slick as rain on a disowned motorway,
Sick as a witch shoved into her own oven
Dreaming of the next double decker, all those
Caged elephants and parrots plotting escape.
Why is broccoli so disgusting, tiny forests
That they are, tempt me instead with cake,
Even breadcrumbs and with the love songs
Of collapsing birds trying their best to breed
In gingerbread nests thatched on 5G masts;
Oh how we sobbed for believing the lies
About a nice trip out to gather puffballs.
How could we have been so naive? We all
Ran from famine between fire trees fuelled
By bone hard hunger, we've escaped, I'm sure
But did we ever get to leave in the first place? ⁄⁄

Zombie

The living dead line our street
lying side by side, head to toe.

A crop of long pig, a river of flesh
baking in the sun, wounds washed clean by rain
their skins thinning like October's days
like tall tales spun on the campaign trail.

But this is what they longed for.

This is what they've won, and we
The Unbelievers were forced to play along

so now, if I make any effort to venture out,
to search for food or fuel
to test the air of this half-botched apocalypse
feel the teasing light, trackways of probing winds

I take it all in, let it fill my emptiness
to the brim in a pang of spiderly loneliness

as I tip-toe the spaces between my neighbours
try not to think of who they were

hold my breath, steel my nerves as if
we were all in the primary school hall
playing a game of Sleeping Lions

as if they were Chinese ghosts
from a slapstick kung fu flick
starring Samo Hung or Jackie Chan.

At times like this, it's hard to remember
exactly what life was like not so long gone

when the whole world was just one click away,
when you're face to face with what we've become. ⁄⁄

Going Verdigris

'Good Morning!' All the plants in the back yard greet me in their dialects of green as I emerge from the kitchen into the day's corona. The human illusion of Civil Time has collapsed in our new Remote Lifestyles and I'm tuning into the deeper rhythms, different layers of Earth Time.

A programme on Radio 4, aired on the 29th February (the Ghost Day), informed me of leap seconds – tiny adjustments made to Coordinated Universal Time to compensate for unpredictable irregularities in Solar Time and the Earth's rotational speed which has been slowing down over millions of years, meaning our days are five hours and fifteen minutes longer than they were a billion years ago.

The time I'm tuning into is multiple and stratified, the plants in the back yard hold it between their leaves as they wave at me in greeting, I trip over its lip and down the spiral of a discarded, upturned snail shell, spin in the little loops of its whirlpools, I sidle into it between beats in the drone of a bee, I float over hard pooled concrete like a silent cloud running over the sea.

Invisible messages zip, criss-crossing, through the air in an instant but talking, the forming of words and sending them out with the breath, well that can take all day, and the silences between the restrained syllables are Saharas, vast expanses of shifting sand dunes where meanings erode, where travellers lose their way on their journey from the Addresser to the intended Addressee.

In these longer days of isolation and confinement my speech is patinaed, shedding words like fruit, gone soft and bruised – unfit to eat, so I commune with the plants in their green dialects, scent and touch. I noticed last night that the skin on my feet feels like bark, my fingernails are growing verdant. ◿

And For The Time Being

Until some other arrangement is made the old Gods of the
boondocks shamble around the centre of our towns and
cities having crawled out of the ditches and the drains,
slithered from the Edgelands far off the beaten tracks,
from the suppressed chambers of our cavernous hearts, to
occupy our boulevards and avenues, loiter on the public
benches, in the parks behind locked gates, where we are no
longer welcome.

In the meantime the Community Wardens and patrolling
Police can't see these eldritch beings, their eyes are tuned
to those they suspect of flouting the rules of The Lockdown,
fleshy miscreants who put us all at risk, who dismiss the
motto 'We're all in this together' as something only our
glorious leaders spout to carpet over the fact we're not. The
Community Wardens are zealous in their sweep and scour
of the streets for anything non-indispensable while the old
Gods run amok around them, cutting us down to size.

And for the time being the doors to the places of worship
are bolted, home to stained glass pools and dust motes and
yet the cemeteries remain open, so we may commune with
the dead, stroll between the interred bones, picture our
own names on their stones, catch a glimpse of Grimnir
dangling from an ash tree, Cernunnos lurking in holly
thickets, Bridhid's bright hair in the flame trees, Hel in the
pungency of freshly dug soil.

And for now, all the faceless mannequins in all the empty
shop windows are the only ones who have watched their
return. But I'm sure I'm not alone, among the living, in
perceiving them during our restricted excursions, between
broadcasts of *Loose Women*, the *One Show* and the next
awkward Ministerial Update. ⁄⁄

Popular Streaming

I saw Godzilla this morning stomping around Albert Park puking plumes of white hot flame, scorching the tree I used to climb, Red Riding Hood was feeding breadcrumbs to the ducks from a swan-shaped pedalo on the boating lake, though the park's been locked for the past four weeks due to the world turning Upside Down. I kept my distance, I didn't venture in, but stopped to watch over the railings as she undressed and flung her cape high into the air, there it hung, suspended for an instant, like a splatter of stage-gore from a movie by Sam Peckinpah, before a spurt of Godzilla's fiery halitosis burnt it to a blackened crisp. She stretched her lips and screamed at the sky, "Why would I trust the wolf?" I rubbed my eyes and looked around, not another soul about, everyone else was holed up at home, social distancing, hooked to the stream of fantasies flowing from their TV screens. ⁄⁄

Castaways

One month in and there's a slow normalisation to the ghost lives we lead, to the sudden drops into unexpected pockets of nothingness while Spring unfolds and spreads her arms wide scattering new colours all over the place. It's like we are living behind a veil, the world in its full complexity is there but we can't connect to it, like we've been emptied out and our pasts are just tall tales we liked to weave into patterns to impress or beguile, but now we're lacking an audience. Future tense phrases of: I'm going to..., shall we make a plan... and why don't we... drift like pink blossom across thinned out pavements, and the present is a precarious ice bridge over a crevasse.

I wake surprised to find you still here after troubled dreams of wandering the beaches of Más a Tierra and hiding away from undead pirates, but like Crusoe it's necessary to chart the territories of our new lives, establish routines and look for footprints in the sand. There is a calmness to be found in letting some things float away on the tide. The passage of weeks is marked by the ritual of communal clapping. Yet there are moments when you're sleeping through recovery when I think I'm only imagining you've come back, and my sense of reality has melted like candle wax.

All the while we try to sieve out the lies and deflections, wade through the deceptive stream of war metaphors, weigh-up whatever morsels of truth we can find and lay them out on the rocks to dry, to sustain us until the worst is over. Some say that this isn't the time for questions, yet the number of fatalities rise and vulnerable heroes move among us, a skeleton crew on our beautiful shipwreck. The horizon line remains flat and featureless, and when a ship does eventually appear there's a nagging suspicion it could be a Man-O-War or a Slaver. ⁄⁄

Fugue
(After Sean O'Brien)

Are we nearly there yet, how much further
To see this dreary river you offered as a lure, which you
say
I crossed once already, when, and why can't I recall it
There is such a fog in my head, it shrouds my thoughts

Did we drink too much last night, weren't you once my
lover
Let me sit on this step for a while to shake off this fugue
And I give you my word I'll not slip your string from my
wrist
Although the melody calls me back down the staircase

Do you hear it too all of those voices behind us beckoning
For clarity although answers are forever deferred
To the end of any composition I'm sure you know that
Mister musician with your song book and lyre

If only you'd turn around and show me your true face
Look into my eyes and assure me this trip is worth it
That we're allowed to travel beyond the local
That this outside you talk of is more than make believe

Sit with me a while and explain why I should leave
This everywhere to exist in just one place in space
Confined to one life in the passing of time
Will you tell me again about this pain you call 'love'. ⫻

Dis-May

As beautiful as ever it was –
with its clouds of hawthorn bloom,
white lace shawls of wild garlic
spread over the banks of the burn,
the fermenting orchestra of birdsong,
the soothing warmth on the skin; and
our reduction in physical contact
due to our learning to live remotely
makes the ache of its fleeting
all the sharper; for like small
excitable dogs we feel the tug
to be everywhere all at once,
sniffing, rubbing, running to and fro
here and there, taking it all in,
but restrained by the knowledge
that we can't, that we might just
be carrying something deadly
inside us – so many have succumbed,
and so we have self-secured
our instincts with leashes that chaff
at the raw skin at our necks,
throttle us in case we should momentarily
forget, go feral, make a dash for it,
head off to visit our favourite
beauty spots, find solace in company
of friends and of loved ones, and so
we forgo these comforts for the sake
of the greater good. We are not heroes,
just ordinary folks struggling to live
during extraordinary circumstances
not one of us has known before,
and so to discover that this Spring
is fully open to some to relish

as they will, though not so for us
who must, above all, follow the rules,
you can hardly be surprised
by the outpouring of resentment
by the rage of being betrayed
by being taken for a docile herd. ⁄⁄

Petrified Citizens

In these days before excavation we are learning to exist inside the sarcophagi of cooled rock. For hours I'll sit, seemingly fossilised, maintaining my asana like a mystic yogi, feeling the weight of earth pressing in upon me, holding me tight like a good mother should.

Hours, days, weeks, months and years slide away, and against enforced inactivity I sense the planet's spin around the sun. The fiery eyes of Medusa still fill my mind's eye, lava bright and exploding; magnificent, it was, how the sight itself was a fishing line dropped into my own liquidity, which snared and extracted my skittery will to move and like a solar flare bleached the colours from me.

Ash is breath. Scorched clinker is flesh. Bones are porous pumice. Hair and nail and facial expressions burnt away in the initial blast. Our shadows were pinned to the walls.

And yet, our encased lifestyles go on remotely, we're busy-busy-busy, being stone. Stolen for centuries from plain sight. But are we not marvels, survivors who did not survive yet remain intact longer than those who did? We endure, and wait for the archaeologists to arrive and break through the crust of our isolation. They will exhume our Golem grammar, measure the rate of our beautiful metamorphosis, hypothesise over our closely held tragedies, finding curious parallels with their own suspect agency and make gallows-jokes about 'stiffs' to dismiss their own mortality. ⫽

Time Dilation

Sitting
at the desk
in the house I realise
both the house and yard beyond
the window (guarded by three carved
wooden elephants) are floating in a soap
bubble, how the membrane is far from constant,
but wobbling and expanding, refracting light, reflecting
it back and how I am caught up in these infinite prisms
that compose the soap bubble's kaleidoscopic interior,
that constitute, even, the notion of self in relation to
everything else, which is nothing but light bouncing
back and forth within the curvature of my bubble
all those darting frequencies of me following
endless arrivals and departures repeated
repeated and repeating with my
hauntings haunting the
haunted

guarded by three carved wooden elephants
who remember
remember
remember ⫽

Glitch

Bamboo, a backcombed explosion
of jade green blades slicing
the warm Summer air in a race
to cram the corner of our back yard
shoot higher than the wall, catch
a breath of breeze to tremble.
It forms a dense curtain –
the start of a forest where a tiger
squats guarding the black path
that leads to The Palace of Endings,
its amber eyes watch as I hang out
the washing with crocodile pegs,
I tell myself they're just snail shells,
the low, rumble-purr is a plane
circling in to land, the black path
is nothing but the soil-stack,
and The Palace of Endings
deep in that bamboo forest
can wait till I'm ready to visit. ⁄⁄

The Strong Silent Type

"Nostradamus and Notre Dame. It's two different things
completely."
    Tony Soprano

"...a vast image out of *Spiritus Mundi* troubles my sight"
    W.B. Yeats

A Tony Soprano look-alike takes a long lick
of his Lemontop while paddling in the shallows,
he's holding on tight to his little boy's wrist

our caporegime squints toward a future
he thinks lies just over the horizon but
the Boss of the Seagulls has swallowed it

though there's no way Tony can know it yet;
so, Bada-bing sits in the belly of this gull
as uncomfortable as a burnt-out cathedral

the little boy steals a pebble from a wavelet
and holds it behind his back like a secret
while Tony stares out his black-out finale

ice-cream trickles over the ring on his finger
and one drop of vanilla falls into the sea,
his boy babbles prophesies at the clouds

where the Boss of the Gulls regurgitates a strip-
club then reels round wide to eye up Carmella's
greasy carton of cod & chips with mushy peas. ⁄⁄

God Falter Hill

This is where deities hesitate and catch their breath, knowing to go any further is to risk too much exposure for they would have to put on people skins and they never make a perfect fit. The town sprawls before them across the basin, the lattice work of roads and streets, the tower blocks, the bridges, the cooling towers and slim chimneys, the river and the sea, where ships slide like snails across the blue.

Down there commerce governs all decisions, the goings and comings and exchanges of word and touch, riding a carousel of perpetual crisis that has gifted us a motto of collective identity, 'ERIMUS'.

Yet leaf-gods loiter at the edge of the treeline telling stories of the lives we might have led had we but stripped off our skins and burned our bones in a ceremonial conflagration. They invite us into the woods to stroll the snaking pathways where snapped branches spell out our nicknames, petnames, usernames and passwords.

The woods take parts of us in, store little souvenirs of our beings in vines wrapped around the bark of oak and beech, we are watered by dew, suckled on sap and soothed into growth by bluebell chimes and the piping chatter of small quick birds. As we take ourselves home, back down the bank into the town-scape, our homunculus left-overs quiver and seep, evolving into the next pantheon of godlings to loiter at the treeline, clacking mandibles and scratching charms on the sky's soft underbelly with the sharpened tines of their antlers. ⁄⁄

At The Heart of this Sick Rose

The boy's gaze grows glassy, yawns fill his little skull, stretch
his lips and jaw wide enough to suck in all he doesn't yet know,
it cools his brain, sets his eardrums fluttering like bat wings,

pleasant lands charge toward him as the miles roll on by,
motion-flicker doodles drawn in each corner of the page,
there is something else in the car with him and Mum and Dad –

not the music from the radio nor the bulletins on the measures
everyone is duty-bound to take, that's why the road's so empty,
Mummy is not feeling too well, she may be one of those ones

that goes to heaven. Is she doing more or less than sleeping,
the boy has been studying her watery reflection in the window
the sickness lives on our bodies and loves to get inside of us,

sleepyhead all this long way, Daddy is driving somewhere safe,
no need to worry, no one can touch us, not a soul come close,
and once Mummy is not dead he shall play King of the Castle

there are blind moles in Daddy's eyes but he has wonderful
water-repellent feathers, there shall be no apologies because
everything can be explained as reasonable, the boy's the key –

for a degree of sympathy, off the hook, our freedoms unlocked,
the rest can be shrugged off, tossed away on the howling storm
there is nothing more to say, so he will not be marked down

for any acts of love, for who among you wouldn't do the same?
Granted, there's always a price to be paid for butchering trust,
it'll be stone-faced heraldries attending pedigrees in a rose garden. ⁄⁄

Ragwort Lore

Oh, persistent weed on our backyard wall, with your roots clinging to the interior of cracks in weathered mortar, your yellow hydra heads held high on slim sun-stretched necks, waiting each morning for the first rays to top the opposite ridge tiles, your leaves outstretched to cup the warmth and catch the cooling wind as you stare in multiple directions; into my kitchen as I wash a pan in the sink, into my neighbour's back room where he sits playing his Xbox and growling like a hound, into the cobbled alleyway where rats nose the rubbish bins, into the yard where the piebald tabby sleeps on the window sill, and more, for our parallel worlds brush against each other like complementary yet incompatible substances, the air against the glass of the kitchen window, the tenancy of each small backyard personalised by arrangements of objects in a temporarily unique constellation of atoms.

Oh, little king of the boundary with your sweet golden crowns, reigning over the old Irish Quarter of pale virgins and Hail Marys, where rosaries count the days since the last confession, ...*forgive me Father*..., where hearts are weighed against a pure white feather. Where the factory girl bites her inner cheek and cradles a new weight in her womb as Granddad's pigeons tumble home like soft rolling prayers, where her only son will ride his tricycle to the court of The High King in Meath to ask for a cure to his stammer, and be gifted a hornet to keep under his tongue. Where Sitric Silkbeard sells repaired washing machines and bags of skunk from a stable of smoke and soapsuds, where he watches the beat of the three women Street Wardens, suspecting *Mór-Ríoghain*. One day they'll alight at his double doors, preening the quills of their dark calligraphy, and ask if he remembers "What hast thou done?" ⁄⁄

Through a haze of pungent bud-smoke Silkbeard and his Manxmen will pay tributes to The Crowned Emperor of Backyards, The Grand Duke of Spilled Bin Bags, begging forgiveness for once slaying the raven. Where Fairy Liquid bubbles brim over the rim of the bowl in a tidal wave of daydream, and the little ragwort on the wall goes on dancing to it all... ⚏

Re-enacting the Armageddon

Through the brick wall, the bark and grumble
of the Dogman's daily, late-night tantrum,
Ogh, for fuuuckssaaake! Can't fuucking believe it!
With muffled snatches of The Yellow Submarine,
and whiskey held, for as long as you can stand it,
burning in the puckering hollow of your tongue;
the oom-pah rhythms of the jaunty carnival song,
blowing bubbles through a straw, *Till we found*
a sea of green – all this nonsense fills you up
inflates you like a helium balloon –

so you swallow the fire water, feel its passage
down your throat, molten gold, lava pouring
down a mountain's fissures, to char villages
with people, dogs fleeing, chickens flapping
in red raw pandemonium, *Ffuuuckssaake!* ⁄⁄

In Extremis

We have a new app to erase you from the death toll, to
alleviate the obvious embarrassment your passing has
caused and to avoid any overly awkward questions that
may penetrate the filter system; which wipes clean the
smudge of your presence from history by applying a few
repeated pixels from the background to camouflage your
absence so only those who look extra carefully would notice
anything amiss, and with everyone distracted by the speed
of the feed, by the fear of the spread, by the fires already
raging over the curve of the horizon, it's highly unlikely to
be noted – your little life will hardly be missed; without a
synecdoche to hang it on or a billboard campaign with a
catchy slogan remembering will fade and the traces of
individual stories will sink into a tide of collective grief
which can be massaged through metaphors of heroes and
villains, muggers, shirkers and Herculean efforts. ⁄⁄

The Unmoving

And still some refuse to budge,
their taproots sunk into the clay of the past,
gripping with the generational surety of bloodlines
onto the density of the Underlands;
onto cooled basalt plugs, coal seams
honeycombs of limestone, onto flint and marl;

they stand steadfast as statues in defiance
to changes riding on the backs of trade winds,
while millions have already lost their foot-hold
and swirl like snowflakes in the Helm,

individuals rendered invisible by their multitudes
all their questions coalescing into an indecipherable howl
from somewhere beyond the well-tended edges
in the wilds outside of the rose garden walls,

while inside the perimeters of fenced communities
the shift in seasons is a matter for sun-block
or cardigans, for devising methods
of keeping the worst of weathers at bay.

So today, let's have a BBQ on the lawn
while the good summer lasts, and forget all the myths
that might move us as the sun hurtles headlong
through space at 200 km per second dragging
its gaggle of infants in an ellipse of 250 million years. ⁄⁄

Nowhere, South Gare

Here, the river becomes the sea,
both gnaw on crumbled concrete
that breaks the waters,
and makes the last distinction
before the senile Tees gives up its ghost.

The rush of waves and the swell
of a cargo ship passing,
heading out into the open flux
of tides and cloudscapes toward
a continent we've sailed away from.

The beach sweeps in a curve
toward Coatham, the rusting silences
of the blast furnace dominates the skyline.
Slag heaps still stinking.

Beyond, the ghetto of green fisherman's huts;
the dunes' sharp grass that can slice the skin,
leave red-raw weals on calves and thighs.

Our Mam used to bring us here to play
when we were kids, we'd pretend to be
marooned pirates searching for treasure
or time travelling dinosaur hunters
before settling down for a picnic
in a hidden hollow of sand.

Now, while this pandemic rages
across the world this post-apocalyptic
landscape seems much more real
than the uncannily emptied town centres
the quiet duel carriageways,
suburban houses all marked by rainbows
instead of a white cross daubed on each door. //

The Atrocity Parade

"Pleasure only starts once the worm has got into the fruit, to become delightful happiness must be tainted with poison."
Georges Bataille

Given the green light the inhabitants of Gomorrah flocked out of their coops to take the air and realign themselves with space, with the distances they had craved for months and they filled the public spaces that had been abandoned, except for their imaginings that had populated the boulevards, the promenades, the plazas in their stead, bloated and hyperreal versions of themselves living their best lives while the physically vulnerable versions dwelt in their enclosures. But now, the warnings and careful measures could be dismissed with a Gung-Ho-Geronimo charge into the invisible hail of infectious bullets that can take a fortnight to penetrate.

The crowds were lapping it up, bolstered up by the soundbites of 'Heroes' and 'Blitz survivors', the true horror of the situation blocked from their minds by denial and cognitive dissonance. She watched from inside her own skin, which she clenched tight about her to avoid contamination, as the parade swept through the streets in a tide of blood, smiling, indignant, exuberant, yelling and demanding freedom. The V.E. Day footage broadcast only last week pulsing like ingested parasites inside their heads. The isolation ravaged architecture of their bodies disguised behind the bright day-glow logos, the photo-shopped images on tee-shirts and hoodies, like the facades over the front of the virtual shops they streamed past on their protest.

She remembered the Body Worlds exhibition she had once seen, the grotesquely beautiful works by Angelina Whalley and Gunther von Hagens, those plastinated, skinned, dismembered cadavers in such ordinary living poses: ⁄⁄

jogging, fishing, reading, their insides turned out in a carnivalesque autopsy. She remembered the uncomfortable sexual stirrings of walking amongst the necromorphs with their landscaped organs and curated skeletons, and now seeing the jubilant highly strung populous celebrating their reclamation of space, their right of connection to the collective, she recognised similar erotic revulsions in the surety that some were walking brazenly to their deaths, committing to become corpses before the Summer was out.

Shaking off the momentary impulse to masturbate she fled to the relative emptiness of the beach, and breathed in the salt-sea air under a sky grown grey with the threat of a storm. 'Don't look, don't look', she told herself. There was no option of going back. ⁄⁄

Post Pandemic Cabinet Briefing

Pinched and pitted faces around an oil-drum brazier. The familiar stink of the nearby river and a mountain range of reclaimed bricks, icy to the touch, their breaths are muddled speech bubbles and the talk is all about what should be done and more importantly when. None of these men are experts, if they were they wouldn't be here, each of them has been juggled around from pillar to post in shuffle after reshuffle, each time applying their instincts of self-preservation and their stubborn will to ride out any difficult situation. Besides, expertise is a discredited thing of the past. What matters now is controlling the narrative.

The flickering light from the fire washes across the mud, the puddles and the foothills of the bricks. The men keep their backs to the slopes, making a tight circle around the rusty drum. But over the shoulders of the one standing opposite they can catch what looks like dumped bodies among the rubble, an arm here, there a protruding knee, soft, fleshy lumps in the darkness. But it is better not to be seen to be looking beyond the circle. Keep it tight. Maintain the appearance of unity. Never acknowledge mistakes.

The firelight plays tricks with their poker faces, making zoomorphic masks. One resembles a lizard, another a wolf, there are hyenas, a gorilla, a cobra, several parrots, foxes, a ram and a bear. They're all driven by their natures, their upbringing, and their sense of status. No one should think they would be capable of acting otherwise, like the scorpion hitching a ride across the river on the back of a frog.

"Didn't we promise to get this thing done?" says one.

"But our own survival does depend upon the herd," someone else mutters into the flaming oil drum.

"All of them?" Says another, "There's long been the need for a cull."

"This," replies the first, "is our best chance to rebuild and restock. We have a brave new world to make."

Each of these creatures considers himself above the law. Their positions, birth rights and super injunctions have long protected them from close scrutiny of their lives. A peeling billboard beside the bus stop at the end of the known world shows the torn figure of Jonny Depp sitting in front of a campfire, a bottle of Sauvage by his side, his cheekbones are rugged rock formations in the dry Arizona desert. Beneath the brand name of the perfume is the legend 'WE ARE THE LAND'. ⫽

Which Disaster Shall We Play Today

Flicking through the available genres to reconfigure the day's tropes took longer than expected, you know what it's like when you can't decide just what it is you fancy experiencing, and most of what is acceptable you've done before in one form or another as endless remakes and spin-offs, and what you haven't might take you deep down a rabbit hole to some place you wouldn't want traceable and where you might not be able to wholly return from. The stock write-ups of the story-lines weren't much help either. *"Haven't we already done that one, sure I've done that to death, maybe I did it once when you had an early night?"*

Although the street was quiet it wasn't gloriously sunny with happy neighbours smiling and waving on their door steps, but slightly overcast and the bin men had wheeled the metal bins out from the alley onto the kerb, ready for the truck to do its rounds. No sign of it yet. Leaves hung heavy on the trees, a gull sailed over the rooftops, a car door slammed shut out of shot, everything looked rosy, and one of the bin men, as eternally young and handsome as James Dean, would be riding the back of the truck in dungarees and a white tee-shirt (of all things) as it rumbles through the estate. It felt like a girl meets zombie, falls in love with zombie, zombie eats girl kind of day.

A group of teenagers hung out in the little urban park, sharing smokes and ribbing each other, bickering about how best to survive the disease, how to rid the town of its scourge. Suddenly one looked up with wide Mickey Rooney eyes to say, *"Hey, why don't we put on a show!"*

"Right here? Right now!" said his girl, a Syrian refugee, and they broke off into a charm song to beguile an invisible audience. ▨

There were the early signs of the destruction to come, overlooked or routinely ignored: a short circuit caused a small fire in an apartment block, an astronomer figured out that a comet was on a collision course with Earth, but suffered a heart attack and died, in the cemetery a flock of starlings attacked a small dog en mass while its owner called it to heel – poor Prince didn't stand a chance against the swarm of airborne piranhas and then there was the scream when she discovered the stripped carcase beside the War Memorial. The sprinkler system in the stairwell failed. Someone smelled smoke and checked their toast wasn't burning.

A cabinet minister, who drew the shortest straw, appeared on TV to report that everything was under control, there was no reason to believe the situation would worsen, the country was a world leader in dealing with circumstances like this, they were being led by the science and everyone should be proud of the response so far. Safety measures would be announced in due course. *"In the meantime"*, she said, *"it's a beautiful day, the beaches are open and people are having a wonderful time."*

A black, vintage car with tinted windows came cruising up the street, causing curtains to twitch. It stopped with its engine running outside of your house just long enough for The Big Man in the back seat to check if you were home before it pulled off and round the corner. We both have the feeling it won't be long before its back.

Little Danny suffered a series of disturbing premonitions and flashbacks. He wanted to show me his butterfly collection including the killing jar but I locked myself in my room to finish my novel. I did not want to be disturbed.

The care worker visiting Margery couldn't control her dry tickly cough. She'd had a sleepless night of flushing which she'd put down to the menopause because there was no way she could afford not to go to work today, not with

Jonny out of a job and the bills stacking up. In the city centre one of the protesters was shot and the march disintegrated into a riot, the looting began. The inferno erupted. The comet crashed into the sea sending tsunamis stampeding toward landmasses. As expected all hell broke loose.

You gave up on the idea of finding anything decent, took a bath to block out the mayhem, to sooth your raw nerves. An hour later I broke through the bathroom door with an axe to find you delirious in cold water and shook you awake to say, *"You're going to get out of this...you're going to go on and you're going to make babies and watch them grow and you're going to die an old lady, warm in your bed. Not here...Not this night. Do you understand me?"*

But all you could say in response was, *"I can't feel my body."* ⁄⁄

A Song for Re-Emergence

When they said it was once again safe to venture outside
we crept from our dens to see what the world had become,
in our absence – at least some of us did,

others had already changed too much,
become over-accustomed to confinement
some had withdrawn their outer limits
into their own internal organs and resembled strangely
beautiful flowers of the sea
their polyp bodies locked onto their sofas and easy chairs,
their tentacles doing the touchy-feely reach and retraction,

but those among us that did emerge saw that our histories
no longer fit their frames,
whatever sureties they'd once contained
had cracked the casings from the inside
spilled, unruly, from the past to the present:

old shoes, odd socks, hand-me-down straight-jackets

and we saw that we no longer sat at the centre of things;
microscopic angels with fiery crowns floated between us
shunting us off into our own peripheries
where we were rendered aliens to our own life stories.

Granted, the air was definitely clearer, star-charged and
on some days it felt more like water – as in
water within a waterfall that had suspended its tumble
and the future was anyone's guess;

of course we were all expected to act
as if everything had gone back to normal,
so we wrapped up our griefs in cellophane,
got back in our cars and repopulated the roads
to make up for the lost miles
to outrun the inevitable blame-game,

but it was difficult to differentiate our own voices
from the conversations of birds, bees, butterflies
and the wagging green tongues of trees, which
during the long months of isolation we'd tuned into
and could not turn off with a simple flick
of a switch or a sign spelling 'Go'. //

Popping The Bubble

"Bubbles in a tube smaller than a millimeter wide appear to
retain no "memory" of the details that led to the break."
  Amir Pahlavan

Who really expected anything else, by which I mean
you don't have to be a 21st Century Nostradamus
to suspect the day would all end in tears, how
midway through a conversation about the weather
and the wish for a holiday abroad somewhere
maybe Ibiza or Tenerife, some place sunny at least,
because you deserve it – especially after the year we've had,

you remember over the bevelled lip of the pint glass
you said you wouldn't do this, wouldn't be caught dead in fact,
just like you once claimed that you would never-ever
become your dad and yet the resemblance grows
like bamboo shoots almost overnight, and you hear him
in the words that stick now in your craw or fall flat into the drink
without as much as a splash to disturb these wary celebrations

and inside it there's a twinge of forgiveness toward him
now that you've learned the trick of turning his skin into glass
so you can watch the regular pump of his human heart,
although in yourself there is only the tang of disappointment
because we do unknowingly what is expected even
and in spite of our best efforts of rebellion. The jukebox

is playing *Cosmic Dancer*, don't we both love this track,
and then you're free-falling from the bevelled lip of the glass
down toward the foamy head of the draught like it's a snowfield
or a torn feather mattress or a handful of his whitened hair. ✍

The Boozer Through The Looking Glass

*"But I don't want to go among mad people," Alice remarked.
"Oh, you can't help that," said the Cat: "we're all mad here.
I'm mad. You're mad."*
    Lewis Carroll

This pub is not the pub we know, though I've sunk pints
here since I was underage and studying at Art College. One
of the regular jokers behind me in the queue to approach
the bar is bemoaning the new regulations meant to keep us
all safe and create the illusion of control, *'Oh remember
when you'd go to the boozer with a big beamer on your face
to see all your mates?"* He's not impressed by what we've
lost.

I order beers, though it takes a while due to a shortage of
choice, and take the glasses outside to our socially
distanced table. Wouldn't it be nice to sit on the grass, but
that's not allowed. Covid must be creeping through the
bright green blades or lurking behind the trees, and we're
not allowed to stand up or move around whilst drinking
because Covid will spot us like a sniper and target us for
sure, but if we sit and speak quietly it's more likely to
overlook our presence. It is important to remain subdued.

Nevertheless, it's nice to sit and chat and have a laugh,
and take and post a group selfie to prove we are there,
we've made it through so far. Each of us are coping with
change, trying our best to navigate the unforeseeable. One
of us is in the middle of a break-up and setting a new
course. *"I'm going to get through this!"* he tells us.

"Course you are mate!" says another who is well used to
rolling with the waves, and picking up and pritt-stiking her
heart back together.

I notice the faces of dead friends in my glass of stout, one extra from today – the phone call still echoing in my ears and the sudden absence of him in the world, him of all people – who was always so much larger than life, makes the afternoon seem like I've strayed into a fairground's Hall of Mirrors.

Look, there we are, isn't that us? Funny creatures locked inside the frames of an elongated and distorted version of reality, aquarium selfies haunted by the memory of how it should have turned out in a world that made some sort of sense, but lost their bearings and slipped down a rabbit hole. I'm wondering who we'll become this side of the looking glass, what masks we'll need to wear.

"Have you been the toilets yet?" one of us says, returning and sitting down swiftly so Covid doesn't spot him. *"There's only one open for the whole pub and it's like Ninja Warrior to get in there. Anyway, fancy another one? I'll get the next round in."* I tell him I'll have another stout and then we toast our departed selves. ⁄⁄

Keening

Because for the time being
the rain has stopped and each room
      of the house is a dumb whirlpool
I take the path beside Bluebell Beck,
deep standing water and mud
      have deterred other travellers,
there's a deceptive distance
within this thin crease that cuts
      through estates from the bound centre
out towards the perimeter, the brown beck
chugs and wallows, reflecting density,
      clouds patterned by gulls, laced by
searching twig-tips, my tyres plough
through the sludge, my daughter's sobs
stinging my ears, it's her day to feel
the weight - or the weightlessness -
of being set adrift on days that have lost
      definition, she said it felt like grief,
so I told her it was natural and good
to mourn the loss of contact, the easy
      cuddle and the kiss on the cheek
with those you love, the smell of skin
the firmness of a held hand, the winding
      beck sings and dances between trees
that wear heavy sleeves of bright moss,
I think they're voguing in a foregone frolic
so stop to view the imperceptible creep,
stroke one damp branch as if it were
the arm of a dear friend or family member
      who exists in a different bubble,
no, I don't cry but the sigh that escapes
my lip is ragged and raw, I watch
      it go flitting, trilling, through foliage
flashing its blood-stained burning breast. ⁄⁄

Landscape of The Flesh
(for Kev Howard)

i

Nightfall to daybreak
cockcrow to afterglow

and all the seconds between
navigate our life-lines
through brawn and brain
through thought and thew

a wind   a flame
an eddy   a wave
inscribe their names
        upon the corporeal.

ii

Come, follow the script, the subtext, plot
through consanguinean territories
      of lineage and legacy.

How can you not?

Pace those scree paths, earth furrows, scar tracks
climb hillock, flint scarp, bone crown, stone crop;

vista upon vista
in a commonwealth of flesh.

iii

How we quarry the good stuff
toss the scrap and slag

grow big and strong on crusts and kernels
grow silky sweet on milk and honey.

Cultivate our inherited homelands,
skeletal shrines of holy wells, ink tarns,
chalk cliffs, soil stacks, lunar lawns.

Tend the termination of our personal turf.

iv

Do we begin or end at our epidermis?
Do our true natures dwell within

these temporary Empires
of meat, bone, marrow, blood?

What beings inhabit our neck of the woods?
Mountain range, sand dune, silt bed, crevasse.

Who squats around the coal heap of the heart
burning embers, sifting ash?

v

These sedimental bodies do not age in time
but hoard the moments that never pass,
we bury them in compacted strata.

We deepen in years.
We thicken in rings.

But what relics do these
terrestrial vessels contain:

all past, present, future within a crook or crease ⁄⁄
the whole of a soul in a fingertip
the spirit coiled inside a follicle
the eternal self in ever-shifting clay? ⁄⁄

Other anthologies and collections available from Stairwell Books

For further information please contact rose@stairwellbooks.com
www.stairwellbooks.co.uk
@stairwellbooks